# The SHELTR Programs



***"Security Hazards – Emergencies – Lethal Threat Response"***

*Published in the United States by*

**America in Defilade, Inc.**

31 March 2025



*Written and Edited by*

American Fulcrum, Inc.



ISBN: 978-1-7346086-5-6

# Table of Opportunities

# Introduction

With the advent of social media and much more sophisticated and rapid lines of communication, it seems every American citizen now has a forum to offer an opinion - warranted, valid, or otherwise. These technologies also afford groups of like-minded Americans the ability to find one another which is creating a lot of noise with no direction.

Through the political and social irresponsibility of our modern day elected officials, the noise that now emanates from the citizens of America is deafening. It is only a matter of time before all of our senses are dulled to the point where we, as an American people, fail not only each other, but the true blessing that is the United States of America.

So now here we are in modern America with all of this noise and no guidance or direction. It is obvious that the only way to ensure America continues to exist is to give guidance to the noise, focusing the noise into a voice of instruction and direction. So how do we create a voice of guidance and instruction for the American people to hear that gives them hope for our future and motivates them to be that great change?

The answer – We Follow the lessons of our American forefathers and create an America for the "American Majority" supporting the goodness in America. By taking the best parts of who we are "now" as a nation we can create the cornerstones of American principles on which to build back our great country. We work as an American people to support what is best for the greater good of us all, the modern American majority, and build our country to that end.

American Fulcrum has created the starting point for building back America by identifying the 12 biggest issues currently facing our modern America and crafting solutions to resolve and manage these issues. To minimize confusion while discussing these 12 issues and proposed solutions, American Fulcrum has put everything in a single book so each issue can be easily referenced for discussion. Some of the ideas and solutions presented by American Fulcrum may seem extreme, but it is the introduction of the idea that begins discussion among the people and sparks the fire of change. The goal of American Fulcrum is to provide a starting point that initiates discussion of the issues facing modern America. By providing structure to the issues, the American people can work more quickly to create an agreed set of solutions that remedy the issues and are supported by the American majority.

With this effort, American Fulcrum is providing guidance to Americans so that they may again hear a voice that provides direction. From this voice, Americans will again begin to take responsibility and accountability of our own individual actions so that we can recognize our weaknesses and our strengths as a nation. It is only by understanding ourselves that we can identify and accept where change is needed.

We must as an American people have the courage to uphold and enforce what we agree is worthy and good. It is not always easy to have courage and do what is right, but the consequences of allowing things to be done selfishly wrong has directly led to the blinding noise in America today.

America only exists because we as an American people choose to make it exist. The resilience of the American people is best defined by our ability to change in order to create greatness. We must now be that great change for ourselves.

It is our opinion that the two (2) greatest issues currently facing the United States of America are Immigration Accountability and Control and the National Security of our Citizens. Detailed below are the proposed solutions for the privatization and reimagination of our current US immigration system and a complete "Unified" system of security programs and protocols for the security of our US citizens.

# Notes

# The SHELTR™ Program

## (Security Hazards - Emergencies - Lethal Threat Response)

Without a doubt, we are moving through some tough times as a country and as American citizens. Unfortunately our schools, work places, entertainment venues and even churches are becoming targets to foreign and domestic terrorism. There simply are not enough law enforcement officers available to secure every location where a terrorist or terrorist organization may attack. It is for this reason that the SHELTR™ Programs were developed. It is vital that the "Defensive Posture" of our American schools, work places and every other place where Americans congregate be stood up to a level that gives us a chance to survive should a crisis or threat engage us. The SHELTR™ Programs give all of us that chance.

The SHELTR™ Programs are the only "Unified", "Non-Lethal" and "Weaponless" security solutions in the world. Our programs are comprised of Training, Defensive Products, Tactical Gear and Mobile Device Applications. Developed by former US Army Special Forces Commanders, US Marine Corp Tactical Police, Law Enforcement, and Emergency Rescue Teams, we have created a total solution that allows our SHELTR Training℠ Courses to be "Design Specific" for any location. None of our programs are generic. Each SHELTR™ Program is designed for the specific environment and space it is meant to protect.

Each SHETLR™ Training Program is conducted by US Military Veterans. All of our Training is specifically designed to provide schools, work place employees as well as anyone attending public events with training, tools and security techniques in which to keep them safe. These tools and techniques teach how to create daily security routines, "LOOK" for things that are out of the norm, "REPORT" incidents in a timely and accurate manner, and "RESPOND" should your campus, work place, entertainment venue or church become engaged by an Active Threat or emergency. Supporting the SHELTR Training℠ Programs are Tactical Defensive Products such as the PAK-JAK™, Blast Board™ and Ballistic Desk™. Also supporting our SHELTR™ Programs are our Mobile Device Applications such as SHELTR Vision™, SHELTR Secure Space™ and MyStudentCare™.

The American people deserve to be safe in our schools, at work and our places of worship. Unfortunately, none of these places are immune to the potential threats posed in today's society. Knowing beforehand how to de-escalate an emergency or threat situation can save lives and lead to fewer serious incidents. If you are not proactive you are destined to become reactive, which is why the SHLETR™ Training Programs are so important. To provide a better understanding, the following pages will provide a brief summary of each SHELTR™ Program.

# SHELTR™ K-12 & SHELTR™ University School Security Programs

The SHELTR™ K-12 and SHELTR™ University School Security Programs provide a "Unified" Security Solution to schools and universities throughout the US. The SHELTR™ (School Hazard-Emergency-Lethal Threat – Response) Program provides on-site "Custom" Training that is created for each specific school, Protective Equipment for every classroom, SHELTR™ Mobile Device Applications (Android and i-phone), and a National School Safety Organization (ENSSA – Educators National School Safety Association) that monitors and manages every SHELTR™ trained school and university.

The SHELTR™ K-12 and SHELTR™ University Security Training Programs are designed to train every teacher and professor, administrative staff, executives as well as all school employees (maintenance, cafeteria, lawn care, etc.). By ensuring every employee at the school is trained to utilize the SHELTR™ techniques and protocols, a more secure and responsive environment is created.

To effectively keep our schools safe, it falls on the teachers, school administrators, staff, students and parents. Everyone must be part of the school security process. The SHELTR™ Program provides a common school security language that allows all of us to work together. Understanding and following the SHELTR™ Program is the only way to strengthen the "Defensive Posture" of our American schools. The SHELTR™ Program allows all of us to work as a community in protecting our schools. Only together will we be able to give our kids a chance to survive should a crisis or Lethal Threat engage their school.

**SHELTR™ School Security Training Program Overview**

SHETR™ Training – (3 Day Progressive Activity)

- 3 Day "On-Site" Activity – K-12 Schools (7-30 Day Activity for Colleges and Universities)
- Day 1 – Coordination with Local Law Enforcement – Fire and Rescue - EMS
- Day 2 – Conduct Individual School Security Assessment – Evade and Evacuation Routes
- Day 3 – Conduct SHELTR Training and School Security Workshop for all teachers and school employees
- Note – Each "Custom" SHELTR™ Program is left with the school at completion of their training

**Upon Completion - SHELTR™ School Security Training Program (2 to 4 week process)**

SHELTR™ Personal Protective Equipment and Gear (See Equipment Brochures in Appendix)

- PAK Jackets™ – Protect a Kid (PAK) Jackets
- TEE Jackets™ – Tornado - Emergency - Evacuation (TEE) Jackets
- Blast Boards™
- Ballistic Desks™
- SHELTR Shield™

**Upon Completion - SHELTR™ School Security Training Program (8 to 12 week process)**

SHELTR™ Mobile Device Applications

- SHELTR Vision™
  - Each School is set up as a "User Group"
  - Immediate Law Enforcement Notification when Activated
  - Immediate School-wide Notification when Activated
  - Immediate School District and State Notification when Activated
  - During an Emergency of Lethal Threat provides "Real Time" video of situation inside the school
    - Location of all Teachers and Students (while on school campus)
    - Location of the Active Threat
    - "Real Time" video of the Active Threat
  - Fire Department and EMS Notification
  - Emergency Locator Transmitter on each registered mobile device

- SPOT™ (Students and Peers Observing Together)
  - Anonymous Anti-Bullying Solution
  - Students can report school infractions or bullying – equalizes student power
  - Students can capture video and Audio using their mobile devices
  - "Student in Crisis" Alert Button with Tracking
  - Angel Line – Suicide Prevention (Anonymous and Text Based Solution)

- MyStudentCare™
  - Parent – Student – Teacher web based Portal
  - Multiple modules allow the automation of daily tasks
  - Communication portal during school emergency or Lethal Threat Activity
    - Alerts sent out immediately to all registered users
    - Situational Updates sent out during the emergency or Threat Activity
    - Provides Parents, Community and the Press with situational updates

**Upon Completion - SHELTR™ School Security Training Program (8 to 16 week process)**

ENSSA™ (Educators National School Safety Association)

- State and National School Safety Repository – Created and Managed at State Level
- Links to DOE, DOJ, DHS, National Law Enforcement
- Online Parents and Partners Portal
  - Provides parents, teacher, administrators and school staff with a forum to interact and share ideas.
  - Law Enforcement, School Security Experts, Psychological Experts can conduct webinars and open forums on topics relating to Statewide (National) School Security Initiatives.
- State approved white papers, training materials, books, videos, etc. maintained in ENSSA™
- State approved school security protective equipment logs maintained in ENSSA™
- Sea Turtle as the National School Safety Logo

# SHELTR™ Work Place Safe

Each year, nearly 2 million American workers report having been victims of workplace violence according to OSHA (Occupational Safety and Health Administration). Those at greatest risk include workers who exchange money with the public, delivery drivers, public service workers, customer service agents and healthcare professionals. While these studies suggest growing levels of employee anxiety, awareness is also an issue. Only 45 percent of those employees surveyed knew their employer had a workplace violence prevention program in place. The same survey notes that nearly 30 percent of employees were unsure of what to do if they witnessed or were involved in a workplace violence incident.

U.S. companies face growing concerns about workplace security. Headlines detailing workplace shootings and other types of violence in the workplace have challenged employers to take a closer look at their security policies. But how can employers protect their workplace from threats such as theft, unlawful forcible entry, sabotage, bombings, and active Lethal Threats. After all the primary function of American business is the operation of the business, not security. Regardless, the effect on the American workforce is causing a reduction in productivity as well as employee retention/attendance. When employees do not feel safe, the business suffers.

SHELTR, Inc. has taken all of these things into consideration and developed the SHELTR™ Work Place Safe Program. This program is built on the concept of keeping each individual employee safe in order to secure the facility and facility campus.

The common misconception among corporate executives is their belief that in order to provide a secure environment for their employees they must only secure their facilities. It is no longer just about facility security. In today's work culture, employee security goes beyond the physical workspace. In developing strategic security protocols, we must reverse our mindset. By working to protect the individual employee, the systems and procedures developed will secure the organization and its facilities by default.

**SHELTR™ Work Place Safe Training Program Overview**

SHETR™ Training – (3 Day Progressive Activity)

- 3 Day "On-Site" Activity – Small Businesses, branch locations, restaurants
    - (7-30 Day Activity for manufacturing facilities, warehouses, production plants)
- Day 1 – Coordination with Local Law Enforcement – Fire and Rescue - EMS
- Day 2 – Conduct Building (parking lots, etc.) Security Assessment – Evade and Evacuation Routes
- Day 3 – Conduct SHELTR Training and Work Place Security Workshop for employees and executives
- Note – Each "Custom" SHELTR Training Program is left with the business at the completion of training

**Upon Completion - SHELTR™ Work Place Safe Training Program (2 to 4 week process)**

SHELTR™ Personal Protective Equipment and Tactical Gear (See Equipment Brochures in Appendix)

- PAK Jackets™ – Protect a Kid (PAK) Jackets (NOTE: These are also designed for Adults)
- TEE Jackets™ – Tornado - Emergency - Evacuation (TEE) Jackets
- Blast Boards™
- Ballistic Desks™
- SHELTR Shield™

**Upon Completion - SHELTR™ Work Place Safe Training Program (1 to 4 week process)**

SHELTR™ Mobile Device Applications

- SHELTR Vision™
    - Each Business is set up as a "User Group"
    - Immediate Law Enforcement Notification when Activated
    - Immediate Business-wide Notification when Activated
    - Immediate Corporate-wide Notification – (If applicable)
    - During an Emergency of Lethal Threat - "Real Time" video of situation inside the business
        - Location of all employees at all times (while on business property)
        - Location of the Active Threat
        - "Real Time" video of the Active Threat
    - Fire Department and EMS Notification
    - Emergency Locator Transmitter on each registered mobile device

- SPOT™ (Security Protocols Observed Together)
    - Anonymous Anti-Bullying Solution
    - Anonymous Anti-Drug Sale or Solicitation Solution
    - Employees can report business infractions, bullying – equalizes employee power
    - Employees can capture video and Audio using their mobile device

**Upon Completion - SHELTR™ Work Place Safe Training Program (1 to 4 week process)**

SHELTR CAPE™ (Corporate Awareness for Protected Environments

- Local and/or National Corporate Safety Repository – Created and Managed at Corporate Level
- Links to DOE, DOJ, DHS, National Law Enforcement
- Online Employee, Executive, Contractor and Partners Portal
    - Provides employees, executives, contractors and business partners with a forum to interact and share ideas.
    - Law Enforcement, Security Experts, Psychological Experts can conduct webinars and open forums on topics relating to Security in the Workplace.
- Corporate approved white papers, training materials, books, videos, etc. maintained in CAPE™
- Corporate approved "Non-Lethal" defensive protective equipment logs maintained in CAPE™
- Sea Turtle as the National Work Place Safety Logo

# SHELTR™ Church

With an increase in criminal activity and acts of violence being committed against our houses of worship, the church must become intentional in its efforts to create an atmosphere of awareness and safety. It is unfortunate, but the reality of our society today requires Church Leaders as well as the congregation to prepare for traumatic events such as medical emergencies, a missing child, vandalism, robbery, disturbances and even Lethal Threats. Every ministry, regardless of the size, must be prepared to respond should an emergency, crisis or Lethal Threat invade your house of worship.

SHELTR, Inc. understands the delicate balance required in providing physical security for our houses of worship. We believe the primary mission of our churches must remain the open practice of religion. To obtain this, we have developed the SHELTR™ Church Security Program. To ensure maximum effectiveness, each "weaponless" Program is designed for your specific house of worship. Our Program concentrates on integrating the "Whole of Community – Whole of Church" concept which is designed to interdict threats from every approaching your house of worship. It then continues in its design to provide for every contingent act; up to and including response to an active Lethal Threat. To ensure complete effectiveness, every SHELTR™ Church Security Program is designed specifically for the house of worship and ministry it is to protect. Generic security programs do not work as every church, their parking lots, playgrounds and gathering areas are all different. You must be intentional and confident in the protection you provide or your security Program will fail.

Utilizing the SHELTR™ Church Security Program every member your church is made aware of how to protect their church. On-site training is provided showing how to understand and report an emergency, identify and report suspicious activity, defend against theft, and most importantly how to respond (not react) during a crisis or Lethal Threat situation.

As we continue to make America a safer country for everyone and return our churches to safe havens for our citizens, we must not hide from the truth. In our society today every community, every gathering event and every venue is a possible target for crisis or Lethal Threats. Preparation and practice are the only options to defeat these threats.

**SHELTR™ Church Training Program Overview**

SHETR Training – (3 Day Progressive Activity)

- 3 Day "On-Site" Activity
    - (7-30 Day Activity for ministries with multiple buildings and/or schools)
- Day 1 – Coordination with Local Law Enforcement – Fire and Rescue - EMS
- Day 2 – Conduct Building (parking lots, etc.) Security Assessment – Evade and Evacuation Routes
- Day 3 – Conduct SHELTR Training and Church Security Workshop for Church Leaders and employees
- Note – Each "Custom" SHELTR Training Program is left with the church at the completion of training

**Upon Completion - SHELTR™ Church Training Program (2 to 4 week process)**

Personal Protective Equipment and Gear (See Equipment Brochures in Appendix)

- PAK Jackets™ – Protect a Kid (PAK) Jackets (NOTE: These are also designed for Adults)
- TEE Jackets™ – Tornado - Emergency - Evacuation (TEE) Jackets
- Blast Boards™
- Ballistic Desks™
- SHELTR Shield™

**Upon Completion - SHELTR™ Church Training Program (1 to 4 week process)**

SHELTR™ Mobile Device Applications

- SHELTR Vision™
    - Each Church is set up as a "User Group"
    - Immediate Law Enforcement Notification when Activated
    - Immediate Church-wide Notification when Activated
    - Immediate Corporate-wide Notification – (If applicable)
    - During an Emergency of Lethal Threat – Provides "Real Time" video of situation inside the church or gathering area
        - Location of all employees and congregation at all times (while on church grounds)
        - Location of the Active Threat
        - "Real Time" video of the Active Threat
    - Fire Department and EMS Notification
    - Emergency Locator Transmitter on each registered mobile device

- SPOT™ (Security Protocols Observed Together)
    - Anonymous Anti-Bullying Solution
    - Congregation can report infractions, bullying or suspicious behavior
    - Congregation can capture video and Audio using their mobile device

**Upon Completion - SHELTR™ Church Training Program (1 to 4 week process)**

SHELTR CAPE™ (Church Awareness for Protected Environments)

- Local, State and National Ministry Safety Repository
- Links to DOE, DOJ, DHS, National Law Enforcement
- Online Church Leaders, employees and congregation Portal
    - Provides everyone in the church with a forum to interact and share ideas.
    - Law Enforcement, Security Experts, Psychological Experts can conduct webinars and open forums on topics relating to Security in the Church.
- Church approved white papers, training materials, books, videos, etc. maintained in CAPE™
- Church approved "Non-Lethal" defensive protective equipment logs maintained in CAPE™
- Sea Turtle as the National Church Safety Logo

# SHELTR™ Healthcare

Healthcare security involves protecting not only staff, employees, vendors and visitors but also patients, who are at their most vulnerable. In addition to creating a safe environment, Healthcare Security also has to meet all healthcare rules and regulations established by The Joint Healthcare Commission, HIPPA and NFPA. Staying in compliance with these rules and regulations creates a unique security risk. For example when dealing with a combative patient the healthcare security team and staff must following TJC rules and when securing the facility by locking doors they must comply with NFPA guidelines.

SHELTR, Inc. understands the difficult balance in creating a secure environment where staff and employees are able to conduct daily healthcare operations while maintaining healthcare compliancy. To help our healthcare facilities effectively achieve this balance we have developed SHELTR™ Healthcare.

The healthcare industry is an extremely volatile workplace due to the nature of its business. According to the US Government Accountability Office (GAO), workers in healthcare facilities experience substantially higher rates of nonfatal injury due to workplace violence compared to workers in all other businesses. The U.S. Bureau of Labor Statistics states healthcare workers are more likely to face workplace violence than prison guards and even police officers.

The reason for such a hostile work environment is due to human "triggers" created in the healthcare workplace. The primary triggers of disruptive and aggressive behavior include stress, fear, anxiety, pain and a range of neurocognitive illnesses. Any of these can lead to verbal and physical abuse in the workplace but they are especially abundant in healthcare. Experts rate violence against healthcare workers at up to 12 times higher than rates for any other industry in the US workforce.

Violent events and threats within healthcare settings continue to rise challenging healthcare security teams, staff and employees on how best to ensure their own safety as well as the safety of their patients. The SHELTR™ Healthcare Program provides a "complete" and "unified" solution to the unique security issues found only in the healthcare industry. Our comprehensive solution begins with a SHELTR™ Healthcare

Security Program created for your "specific" healthcare facility. We customize your training program to support the daily operations of your actual healthcare facility. Once your staff and employees have completed their SHELTR™ Healthcare Training Program, our team implements and trains your staff and employees on the usage of our SHELTR™ mobile device security applications. These mobile applications are designed to connect every employee in the facility to ensure constant visibility and communication. The culmination of the SHELTR™ Healthcare Training Program is the distribution and user training of our SHELTR™ "non-lethal" defensive equipment. This equipment is designed to deter threats while working to protect staff, employees and patients.

SHELTR, Inc. understands the primary mission of healthcare facilities is to administer healthcare to our citizens. The SHELTR™ Healthcare Program is the only "complete" healthcare security program in the world specifically designed to provide a secure work environment while allowing the uninterrupted daily operations of your healthcare facility.

**SHELTR™ Healthcare Training Program Overview**

SHETR Training – (3 Day Progressive Activity)

- 3 Day "On-Site" Activity – Small to medium size Healthcare Facilities
    - (7-30 Day Activity for Healthcare Facilities with multiple buildings)
- Day 1 – Coordination with Local Law Enforcement – Fire and Rescue - EMS
- Day 2 – Conduct Building (parking lots, etc.) Security Assessment – Evade and Evacuation Routes
- Day 3 – Conduct SHELTR Training and Healthcare Security Workshop for employees, staff & executives
- Note – Each "Custom" SHELTR Program is left with the Healthcare Facility at the completion of training

**Upon Completion - SHELTR™ Healthcare Facility Training Program (2 to 4 week process)**

Personal Protective Equipment and Gear (See Equipment Brochures in Appendix)

- PAK Jackets™ – Protect a Kid (PAK) Jackets (NOTE: These are also designed for Adults)
- TEE Jackets™ – Tornado - Emergency - Evacuation (TEE) Jackets
- Blast Boards™
- Ballistic Desks™
- SHELTR Shield™

**Upon Completion - SHELTR™ Healthcare Facility Training Program**
**(1 to 4 week process)**

SHELTR™ Mobile Device Applications

- SHELTR Vision™
  - Each Healthcare Facility is set up as a "User Group"
  - Immediate Law Enforcement Notification when Activated
  - Immediate Healthcare Facility-wide Notification when Activated
  - Immediate Corporate-wide Notification – (If applicable)
  - During an Emergency or Lethal Threat - "Real Time" video of situation inside the business
    - Location of all employees at all times (while at Healthcare Facility)
    - Location of the Active Threat
    - "Real Time" video of the Active Threat
  - Fire Department and EMS Notification
  - Emergency Locator Transmitter on each registered mobile device

- SPOT™ (Security Protocols Observed Together)
  - Anonymous Anti-Bullying Solution
  - Anonymous Anti-Drug Sale or illegal solicitation Solution
  - Employees can report Healthcare Facility infractions – equalizes employee power
  - Employees can capture video and Audio using their mobile device

**Upon Completion - SHELTR™ Healthcare Facility Training Program**
**(1 to 4 week process)**

SHELTR CAPE™ (Corporate Awareness for Protected Environments)

- State and National Corporate Safety Repository – Created and Managed at Corporate Level
- Links to DOE, DOJ, DHS, National Law Enforcement
- Online Employee, Executive, Contractor, Partners and Patient Portal
  - Provides employees, executives, contractors, business partners and patients with a forum to interact and share ideas.
  - Law Enforcement, Security Experts, Psychological Experts can conduct webinars and open forums on topics relating to Security in Healthcare Facilities.
- Facility approved white papers, training materials, books, videos, etc. maintained in CAPE™
- Facility approved "Non-Lethal" defensive protective equipment logs maintained in CAPE™
- Sea Turtle as the National Healthcare Safety Logo

# SHELTR™ Shopping

Shoppers, retail tenants, their employees, walkers, food court and restaurant patrons all need to feel secure and welcome in our shopping centers and malls throughout America. Many areas associated with shopping centers and malls have unique security opportunities. Parking lots, parking garages and outdoor shopping venues are just a few of the security challenges present in shopping centers and malls. Each of these challenges must be taken into account when designing an effective security program. A single incident could prevent customers from shopping at your facility. Partnering with the right security organization is critical for ensuring the safety and security of the public and store tenants in your shopping center or mall.

SHELTR, Inc. understands the many challenges that must be overcome in retail security. To meet these challenges we have developed the SHELTR™ Shopping Security Program.

Shopping centers and malls offer some of the biggest venues in America where large groups of people gather to shop, socialize and eat. When large groups of people come together, they are particularly susceptible to security threats. As it relates to shopping centers and malls, these threats include:

- **Theft and shoplifting**
  In 2018 U.S. retailers lost nearly $50 billion to employee theft and customer shoplifting.

- **Vandalism**
  According to the US Small Business Administration, a single incident of vandalism costs on average $3,370.

**Physical altercations**
Confrontations are highest during high-traffic periods – Black Friday, After Christmas Sales, Back to School Shopping.

- **Unauthorized entry**
  With the number of people entering and exiting shopping centers and malls on a daily basis it becomes a difficult challenge to monitor and manage. In addition, deliveries made throughout the day pose a unique security opportunity itself. Procedures and preventative measures must be put in place in order to manage the flow and safety of shoppers, employees, vendors, and deliveries.

- **Automobile-related crime**
  Shopping center and mall parking lots, where vehicles are left unattended and unmonitored for extended periods of time, are prone to vandalism, break-ins, and vehicle theft.

- **Emergencies**
  Although shopping centers and malls are not prone to fires, floods or natural disasters, they do happen on occasion. Every shopping venue must have an emergency evacuation and crisis plan of action in place. As there is no way to forecast when or where an event may occur, several plans must be in place for every area of the shopping center or mall. In addition, plans must be put in place for medical emergencies. As shopping centers and malls are very large, mobile applications should be used for direct communication with police and EMS to provide the quickest possible route to the location of the emergency.

- **Lethal Threats**
  Armed attacks, which have become all too common in recent years, pose a serious threat to shopping centers and malls. The open expanses and large shopping crowds make it difficult to provide quick cover from a Lethal Threat. It is vital that cover locations, evacuation routes and medical aid stations be clearly marked and in abundance throughout shopping centers and malls. In addition, mobile applications that link shoppers, tenants and employees to your shopping center will allow shopping center security to push vital information and updates to everyone in a timely manner. Speed of communication is one of the most important defensive tools when working to move large numbers of people from a threat engaged venue.

Each of our SHELTR™ Shopping Safety Programs is designed specifically to protect your shopping center or mall. We continually study the challenges posed by shopping centers and mall security to ensure we are always providing "Best Practice" solutions in our Program. All training associated with our Program is conducted on-site to ensure your employees and tenants correlate their training with their actual shopping center or mall. Included with your SHELTR™ Shopping Security Program are SHELTR™ mobile applications designed specifically for your venue. These mobile applications are made available to your shoppers, employees, vendors and tenants to provide seamless communication should an emergency or threat occur at your shopping center of mall. Finally, SHELTR™ "non-lethal" defensive equipment and aid stations are made available for your specific security needs. This equipment has been designed to integrate with the SHELTR™ Shopping Program and provides shoppers, employees and tenants with defensive security measures should an emergency or lethal threat occur.

**SHELTR™ Shopping Training Program Overview**

SHETR Training – (3 Day Progressive Activity)

- 3 Day "On-Site" Activity – Small to medium size shopping center
  - (7-30 Day Activity for large shopping centers, shopping centers with multiple buildings, malls)
- Day 1 – Coordination with Local Law Enforcement – Fire and Rescue - EMS
- Day 2 – Conduct Building (parking lots, etc.) Security Assessment – Evade and Evacuation Routes
- Day 3 – Conduct SHELTR Training and Security Workshop for employees, executives, and tenants
- Note – Each "Custom" SHELTR Program is left with the Shopping Center at the completion of training.

**Upon Completion - SHELTR™ Shopping Security Training Program (2 to 8 week process)**

Personal Protective Equipment and Gear (See Equipment Brochures in Appendix)

- PAK Jackets™ – Protect a Kid (PAK) Jackets (NOTE: These are also designed for Adults)
- TEE Jackets™ – Tornado - Emergency - Evacuation (TEE) Jackets
- Blast Boards™
- Ballistic Desks™
- SHELTR Shield™

**Upon Completion - SHELTR™ Shopping Security Training Program (2 to 6 week process)**

SHELTR™ Mobile Device Applications

- SHELTR Vision™
    - Each Shopping Center or Mall is set up as a "User Group"
    - Immediate Law Enforcement Notification when Activated
    - Immediate Shopping Center or Mall-wide Notification when Activated
    - Immediate Corporate-wide Notification – (If applicable)
    - During an Emergency of Lethal Threat provides "Real Time" video of situation inside the Shopping Center or Mall
        - Location of all employees and tenants at all times (while in shopping center of mall)
        - Location of the Active Threat
        - "Real Time" video of the Active Threat
    - Fire Department and EMS Notification
    - Emergency Locator Transmitter on each registered mobile device

- SPOT™ (Security Protocols Observed Together)
    - Anonymous Anti-Bullying and Anti-Gang Solution
    - Anonymous Anti-Drug Sale Solution
    - Employees can report business infractions, bullying, gang activity or solicitation
    - Tenants can report theft, gang activity
    - Shoppers can report bullying, gang activity, witness to a theft or crime
    - Shoppers, Employees and Tenants can capture video and Audio using their mobile device

**Upon Completion - SHELTR™ Shopping Security Training Program (1 to 4 week process)**

SHELTR CAPE™ (Corporate Awareness for Protected Environments)

- State and National Corporate Safety Repository – Created and Managed at Corporate Level
- Links to DOE, DOJ, DHS, National Law Enforcement
- Online Employee, Executive, Tenants, vendors and Shopper Portal
    - Provides employees, executives, tenants, vendors and shoppers with a forum to interact and share ideas.
    - Law Enforcement, Security Experts, Psychological Experts can conduct webinars and open forums on topics relating to Security in the Workplace.
- Shopping Center and Mall approved white papers, training materials, books, videos, etc. maintained in CAPE™
- Shopping Center and Mall approved "Non-Lethal" defensive protective equipment logs maintained in CAPE™
- Sea Turtle as the National Healthcare Safety Logo

# SHELTR™ Events

Events range from political conventions and award shows to the Super Bowl. Regardless of the venue, Event Security entails far more than just providing security personnel. The process of securing any Event is complex and requires extensive coordination and communication regardless of the Event type or venue size. It is vital that any situation at an Event is identified correctly, reported immediately, handled as discretely as possible and as quickly as possible so that other attendees may continue to enjoy the Event. Should it be an active shooter or active threat situation, then prior planning that has been trained and rehearsed is the only option to reduce casualties.

SHELTR, Inc. understands the complexities of Event Security and has utilized their knowledge to develop the SHELTR™ Event Security Program. This unique program provides "Best Practice" security operations in areas such as crowd assessment and flow, emergency/crisis response and control, Event wide communication plans of action and "Threat Identification" – "Threat Response" techniques.

The SHELTR™ Event Security Program ensures the safety of your guests, employees, vendors, athletes and/or talent. Our "non-lethal" Program is designed to keep everyone safe while also protecting the Event venue from property damage. Each SHELTR™ Event Security Program is designed specifically for your individual Event and to secure your specific venue. Our Program concentrates on 5 Key Areas:

1. Pre-Event Coordination
    - Owners of the venue
    - Employees working the Event
    - Event Security
    - Event Vendors and Delivery Teams
    - Local Law Enforcement, EMS and Fire Departments
    - Local and Regional Weather Stations (Outdoor Sporting Events, Race Events, Etc.)
    - State Police (when needed)

2. Pre-Event Walk Thru
    - Identification of risk areas, choke points, hide sites, blind spots, mass congregation areas
    - Identification of Mass Exit Routes (MER's) for emergency exiting
    - Review and confirm venue routine for Entry and Exit locations
    - Establish Security Check points for Entry and Exit locations (As Needed)
    - Review and confirm predicted Crowd Flow for Event-Day activities
    - Establish Crowd Control viewing stations and check points throughout the venue (As Needed)
    - Review and confirm Attendee Communication Plan of Action (Sound, Signs, Lights)

3. Event-Day Activities
    - Event Security Teams Communication Plan of Action
    - Local Law Enforcement, EMS, Fire Communication Plan of Action
    - Emergency Mass-Exit of Vehicles - Traffic Flow Plan of Action
    - Parking Security Plan of Action
    - Crowd Hostility Plan of Action (minimal persons engaged)
    - Riot Hostility Plan of Action (multiple persons engaged)
    - Medical Emergency Plan of Action (inside and outside of the venue)
    - Fire Plan of Action (inside and outside of the venue)
    - Gas/Smoke Plan of Action (inside and outside of the venue)
    - Weather Crisis Plan of Action
    - Active Shooter/Active Threat Plan of Action

4. Event-End Activities
    - Clearing the venue – Confirm "Clear" (Includes all buildings, parking lots, venue roads)
    - Securing the venue – Confirm "Secure"
    - Final Inspection
    - Final Out

5. After Action Review (AAR)
   As many events are recurring and utilize the same venue it is helpful to conduct an After Action Review at the completion of an Event to determine what works and what needs work. The SHELTR™ Event Security Program creates a customized AAR checklist specifically for your Event and venue. This critical function is extremely important when working to create stronger security techniques and procedures for your Event. In addition, by gaining better knowledge of the venue footprint and operations to keep that venue secure, a stronger more cohesive security solution is created.

**SHELTR™ Event Training Program Overview**

SHETR Training – (3 Day Progressive Activity)

- 3 Day "On-Site" Activity – Small to medium size Event and venue
    - (7-30 Day Activity for large venue, outdoor event, races)
- Day 1 – Coordination with Local Law Enforcement – Fire and Rescue - EMS
- Day 2 – Conduct Building (parking lots, etc.) Security Assessment – Evade and Evacuation Routes
- Day 3 – Conduct SHELTR™ Training and Security Workshop for employees, security teams & execs
- Note – Each "Custom" SHELTR Program is left with the Event and venue at the completion of training

**Upon Completion - SHELTR™ Event Security Training Program (1 to 2 week process)**

Personal Protective Equipment and Gear (See Equipment Brochures in Appendix)

- PAK Jackets™ – Protect a Kid (PAK) Jackets (NOTE: These are also designed for Adults)
- TEE Jackets™ – Tornado - Emergency - Evacuation (TEE) Jackets
- Blast Boards™
- Ballistic Desks™
- SHELTR Shield™

**Upon Completion - SHELTR™ Event Security Training Program (1 to 2 week process)**

SHELTR™ Mobile Device Applications

- SHELTR Vision™
    - Each Event and venue is set up as a "User Group"
    - Immediate Law Enforcement Notification when Activated
    - Immediate Event-side Notification when Activated
    - Immediate Corporate-wide Notification – (If applicable)
    - During an Emergency of Lethal Threat provides "Real Time" video of situation inside the Event
        - Location of all employees and guests at all times (while at the Event)
        - Location of the Active Threat
        - "Real Time" video of the Active Threat
    - Fire Department and EMS Notification
    - Emergency Locator Transmitter on each registered mobile device

- SPOT™ (Security Protocols Observed Together)
  - Anonymous Anti-Bullying and Anti-Gang Solution
  - Anonymous Anti-Drug Sale Solution
  - Employees can report business infractions, theft, bullying, gang activity or illegal solicitation
  - Guests can report theft, gang activity, crisis or emergency
  - Guests and Employees can capture video and Audio using their mobile device

**Upon Completion - SHELTR™ Event Security Training Program (1 to 2 week process)**

SHELTR CAPE™ (Corporate Awareness for Protected Environments

- State and National Corporate Safety Repository – Created and Managed at Corporate Level
- Links to DOE, DOJ, DHS, National Law Enforcement
- Online Employee, Executive, Contractor and Partners Portal
  - Provides employees, executives, contractors and business partners with a forum to interact and share ideas.
  - Law Enforcement, Security Experts, Psychological Experts can conduct webinars and open forums on topics relating to Security in the Workplace.
- Corporate approved white papers, training materials, books, videos, etc. maintained in CAPE™
- Corporate approved "Non-Lethal" defensive protective equipment maintained in CAPE™
- Sea Turtle as the National Event Safety Logo

# The SHELTR™ Program
## Products & Gear

An extremely important part of the SHELTR™ Program are the Personal Protective and Defensive Products designed to work with the SHELTR Training℠ Program. These Tactical Defensive Products are detailed on the following pages.

**<u>The PAK-JACKET™</u>** System (www.PAKJACKET.com) is designed to provide individual protection to those engaged in a lethal threat or crisis situation. The PAK-JACKETS™ are pre-positioned in fireproof alarm boxes within classrooms, administrative offices and common areas throughout the school. Should a crisis or lethal threat occur, the PAK-JACKET™ systems are issued to students, faculty and staff. The PAK-JACKET™ provides personal protection while affording the freedom of movement. Features of each PAK-JACKET™

Each PAK-JACKET™ System is built to the following specifications and standards:

- Manufactured to NIJ-IIIA ballistic standards
- Will provide protection from .22, .44, .45 and 9mm ammunition rounds
- Fire Retardant
- Cut Proof - knife and razor blade
- Stab Proof
- Bite Proof

Each PAK-JACKET™ System includes the following for additional protection:

- Kevlar Weave gloves - cut resistant (child and adult)
- "High Heat Intensity" goggles - (child and adult)
- High decibel whistle (also works when wet)
- Vacuum sealed first aid kits - fastened to inside of PAK-Jacket™

**The Blast Boards™** www.BLASTBOARDS.com are white boards that have been manufactured with a ballistic resistant material to provide protection in an active threat or crisis situation. The Blast Boards™ are designed to be installed in classrooms and function like a regular white board. Should an active threat or crisis occur, the quick release system removes the Blast Boards™ from the wall in a few seconds, so they can be utilized as a "bullet proof" barrier.

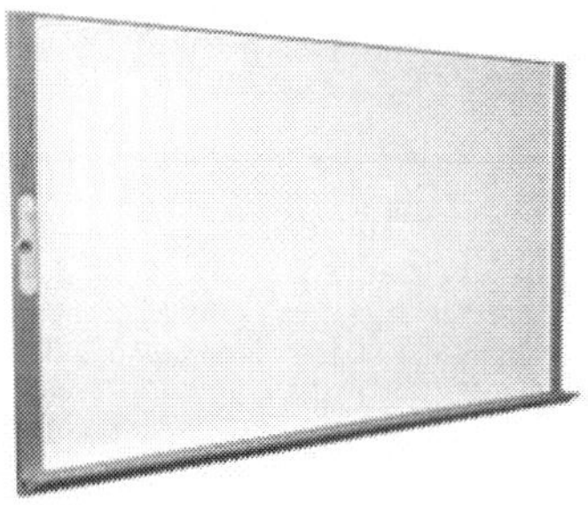

Features of the Blast Boards™ include: Blast Boards™

- Manufactured to NIJ-IIIA ballistic standards
- Will provide protection from .22, .44, .45 and 9mm ammunition rounds
- Can be fastened over an existing chalkboard or directly mounted to any
- surface area
- Each Blast Board™ is mounted with a quick release system that can be
- operated by 1 person
- Lightweight design for ease of movement
- The back of each Blast Board™ has handles mounted so it can be moved
- for mobile protection

**The Ballistic Desk™** System (www.BALLISTICDESK.com) is an armored "desk top" panel that can be fitted over an existing student desk or manufactured as the top of a new student desk. The Ballistic Desk™ panels have been manufactured with a ballistic resistant material to provide individual ballistic protection during a lethal threat or crisis situation. Each Ballistic Desk™ panel has a quick release system that removes it from the student desk base in seconds. Each Ballistic Desk™ panel has hand holds on the back to afford freedom of movement to the individual user.

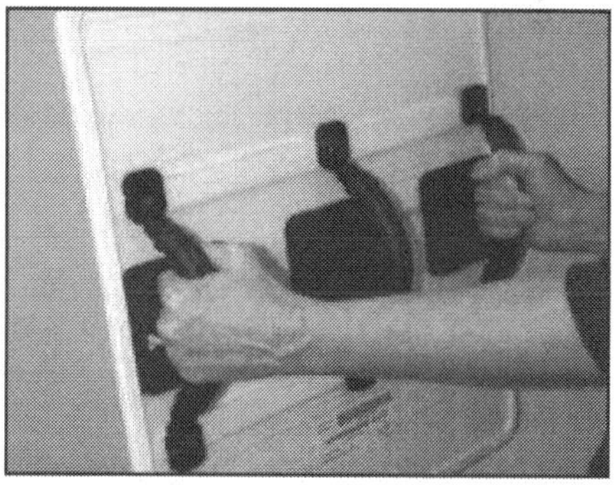

Features of the Ballistic Desk™ include:

- Manufactured to NIJ-IIIA ballistic standards
- Will provide protection from .22, .44, .45 and 9mm ammunition rounds
- Can be fastened over an existing student desk or be manufactured as a desktop to a new student desk

- Each Ballistic Desk™ panel is mounted with a quick release system that can be operated by 1 person
- Lightweight design for ease of movement
- The back of each Ballistic Desk™ has handles mounted so it can be utilized for mobile protection

**The SHELTR Shield™** (www.SHLETRSHIELD.com) is designed to provide individual ballistic protection during a lethal threat or crisis situation. Each SHELTR Shield™ is made of rigid ballistic resistant material and is designed to support the deployment of oleoresin capsicum (OC) spray, which is a chemical agent used to irritate the eyes causing tears, pain and temporary blindness. When employed properly, the SHELTR Shield™ system is a non-lethal threat deterrent tool. The SHELTR Shield™ is available in 3 sizes, one of which fits underneath a standard sized desk used by most US teachers.

Features of the SHELTR Shield™ include:

- Manufactured to NIJ-IIIA ballistic standards
- Will provide protection from .22, .44, .45 and 9mm ammunition rounds
- Armored panels of the SHELTR Shield™ are lightweight
- Ergonomic hand holds with slip resistant grips
- Optional "OC" deployment system
- Stored under a desk for easy employment should a lethal threat or crisis occur

**The TEE-Jacket™** System (www.TEEJACKET.com) provides individual mobile protection during a natural disaster, fire or crisis situation that may occur on campus. The TEE-Jacket should be issued to each IHE student when they arrive on campus to assist the individual students in the event of a crisis or emergency. Each TEE-Jacket is available in various school colors.

The features of the TEE-Jacket™ include:

- Each TEE-Jacket™ is fire retardant, cut proof, razor
- proof, slash proof, and bite proof
- Kevlar weave gloves (cut resistant)
- High heat intensity goggles (forms to the face)
- Vacuum sealed first aid kits attached to the inside of each TEE-Jacket™
- High decibel whistle (also works when wet).
- Nomex IIIA hood to protect the head, face and neck
- region from flying debris and fire
- Fire respirator and smoke hood (optional) inside each TEE-Jacket™

# The SHELTR™ Program

## Mobile Applications

**SHELTR Vision™** (www.SHELTRVISION.com) is a "State of the Art" mobile device application designed to allow teachers and staff to provide "Real Time" situational information to Law Enforcement, Firefighters, and EMS. The SHELTR Vision™ system provides "Real Time" video, sound and location to law enforcement and rescue teams during a lethal threat or crisis situation. When a SHELTR Alarm is triggered, each mobile device implemented with SHELTR Vision™ is activated.
The SHELTR Vision™ system works with an integrated mapping system developed specifically for each school or university to detail each school's building layouts and campus. This mapping system allows law enforcement and first responders the ability to see each activated SHELTR Vision™ mobile device so they know where teachers and their students are located, allowing threat mitigation actions to be employed more precisely.

Features of the SHELTR Vision™ system include:

- Emergency locator beacon
- SHELTR Vision™ alert - immediately notifies everyone in your SHELTR
- Vision™ network of a lethal threat or crisis
- The system works with a customized geo-position system to incorporate
- sports fields, parking lots and common areas
- SHELTR Vision™ works with cellular service or the school's Wi-Fi system

**SPOT™** (www.SPOTSTRONG.com) Students and Peers Observing Together SPOT™ is a mobile device application designed for students to help schools track bullying and other incidents in order for deterrence action to be employed. SPOT™ is an anonymous reporting tool and leaves no record of an "incident reporting" on the user's mobile device. SPOT™ allows users to attach a picture or a 30 second video with the anonymous "incident SPOT™ report" to provide more detailed information about the incident.

Additional features of SPOT™ include:

- The anonymous reporting feature can be disabled by the user if the user
- would like to communicate directly with school administrators.
- SPOT™ is designed with an Emergency Locator Transmitter (ELT) that
- can be activated by the user to receive emergency assistance during a threat or crisis situation.
- SPOT™ is designed with an "Angel Line" so that users who may be
- struggling with life changing situations can reach out for help. This feature can be anonymous or identifiable at the user's discretion.

**MyStudentCare™ (www.MYSTUDENTCARE.org)** (MSC) allows school administrators and teachers to seamlessly and instantly connect with parents to provide information, education updates, and alerts. MSC was designed using a series of interactive information modules and culminated in the "Best Student Services Product" on the market today. We use the term "Student Services" because MSC addresses all of the service areas focusing on students during the school day. MSC Modules reflect the daily activities of teachers, administrators, nurses and principals electronically. It minimizes tedious and consuming "paperwork drills" by transitioning the tasks to an electronic format, increasing efficiency and productivity. An electronic repository replaces mounds of paperwork and the potential for vital information being lost. MSC files can be audited at any time and are 100% HIPAA compliant for security and accountability.

MSC features include:

- A user-friendly interface that is accessible through all portable devices such as smartphones, tablets, netbooks, and laptops.

- Seamlessly Integrates communication with teachers, students, parents and school administrators.
- Automates nearly every daily school business process to reduce duplicate paperwork, increase accuracy and ensure communication.
- Using MSC, parents can also register for school activities such as sports participation, school field trips, class pictures, fundraising sales, etc.
- MSC allows parents to pay for school lunches, school activities and school events right from their phone, computer or tablet.
- MSC provides parents with notifications of their student's activities, school events, upcoming holidays and teacher workdays.
- MSC is also integrated with the SHELTR™ Program to provide immediate notification of incidents, school emergencies or a school crisis. MSC provides "real-time" information to keep parents up to date should any emergency occur at the student's school.

# The SHELTR™ Program
## Software Solutions

**ENSSA™** (www.ENSSAS.org) Educators National School Security Association – Is an organization created to provide a national repository for school security information. The SHELTR Program™ developed the ENSSA Organization in order to create open lines of communication between every person involved in education to include parents, teachers, school administrators, school employees, city leaders, civic leaders, etc.

ENSSA is a "Whole of Community" concept that builds security through information provided to everyone in the community. In addition to being a national repository, ENSSA™ is available to each US state and is designed to network with the national SHELTR Programs™ employed within each US state.

The ENSSA™ system is fully customizable to each US state's Department of Education (DOE) and captures all white papers, videos, forums and SHELTR Training™ that is authorized by the state.

Each state's ENSSA™ system affords their state's Department of Education the ability to promote school safety and security through the dissemination of current "Best Practice" solutions, ideas and experiences.

As a national school security solution, each US state's ENSSA™ system is networked to the national ENSSA™ system for dissemination and receipt of national school security information. ENSSA™ is an extremely powerful tool in our fight against active shooter and active threat deterrence in our US schools.

# The SHELTR™ Program

## Copyrights – Trademarks – Patents – Service Marks

SHELTR, Inc. and American Fulcrum, Inc. utilize Patents, Copyrights, Service Marks and Trademarks to protect the intellectual property rights of their Programs, Products, Gear, Mobile Applications and IT software solutions. The way each works to protect different types of creative work is detailed below:

**Patents** - Protect inventions, such as new tools, products, or processes. There are three types of patents: utility patents, plant patents, and design patents. Utility patents protect how something works, while design patents protect how something looks and feels.

**Copyrights** - Protect original works of authorship, such as books, songs, art, architecture, and music. Copyrights are generally valid for the life of the author plus 70 years.

**Trademarks** - Protect indicators of a company's brand, such as logos, slogans, or business names. Trademarks differentiate a product from similar products.

**Service Marks** - Protect original programs, solutions or services that are created and implemented to teach or improve a task or event. A Service Mark is similar to a Trademark in that it is used to identify and distinguish the source organization of the program, solution or service rather than a tangible product.

Every SHELTR™ Program, SHELTR™ Gear, SHELTR™ Product, SHELTR™ Mobile Application and SHELTR™ IT Solution has been Copyrighted, Trademarked and/or Service Marked to protect the intellectual property rights of all our SHELTR™ suite of products.

Every American Fulcrum™ Program, American Fulcrum™ Gear, American Fulcrum™ Product, American Fulcrum™ Mobile Application and American Fulcrum™ IT Solution has been Copy Righted, Trademarked and/or Service Marked to product the intellectual property rights of all our American Fulcrum™ suite of products.

No SHELTR™ or American Fulcrum™ Programs, Gear, Products, Mobile Applications or Solutions are authorized to be utilized, marketed, publicized, photographed or videoed without the express written consent of SHELTR, Inc. and/or American Fulcrum, Inc.

# The SHELTR™ Program
## Nationwide Community Participation

School security is currently the most critical issue in America. It affects almost every home in our country as nearly everyone is related to a student, teacher, school employee or school administrator. It is for this reason that the citizens of our country are asking to help keep our schools safe. They want to be part of the solution that ends school violence. But currently, there are no major programs available in any US state that accepts the assistance from their citizens. The SHELTR™ Program is different in that it works to facilitate the efforts of everyone in the community:

- Citizens (Parents, Grandparents, Extended Family Members)
- Civic Organizations (Rotary, Shriners, Lions, Boy and Girl Scouts)
- Community Support Organizations (Churches, Temples, Synagogues)
- Corporations and Small Businesses (State and National)

The SHELTR™ Program is a "Unified" school security solution that invites everyone to be a part of the effort. This program gives people something they can see, touch and feel and allows them to finally be part of the solution.

In addition, The SHELTR™ Program is a nationwide school security solution which allows every American to be involved in stopping school violence. By offering this single "World Class" school security solution for the entire country we are able to eliminate confusion from redundancy and guessing from having multiple school safety programs. Having a primary nationwide school security solution allows speed of information to be disseminated and implemented to every school and every community. It also allows students, teachers and parents that may transfer schools to already be familiar with the school security solution as it will mirror the school security program from their previous school. The SHELTR™ program creates a nationwide common effort to finally stop school violence.

- For those that want more direct involvement we offer the "I Provide SHELTR" Campaign.
- Licensed logos will be made available for those that want to merchandise and advertise:
    - Schools (club organizations, sports programs, teacher and administrator groups)
    - Civic Organizations (Rotary, Shriners, Lions, Boy and Girl Scouts)
    - Community Support Organizations (Churches, Temples, Synagogues)
    - Corporations and Small Businesses (State and National)

To give our American citizens something more tangible so they can feel like they actually belong to the effort of ending school violence, the SHELTR™ Program offers Free membership to ENSSA (Educators National School Safety Association). ENSSA is an interactive web portal that contains everything relating to school security for every school in America. As an ENSSA member you are able to follow the security solutions being implemented in your child's school, join chatrooms, participate in online conferences and watch online safety instructional videos. Being an ENSSA member allows every American to:

- Promote and maintain community involvement throughout their state
- Access the Information repository and school security updates in your child's school
- Join blogs, forums, chat-rooms and webinars relating to your state's SHELTR™ school security program
- Ask Question and get Answers from the experts

# The SHELTR™ Program
## American Business Partnerships

It is vital that the "Defensive Posture" of our schools in America be stood up to a level that gives students, teachers and school employees a chance to survive should a crisis or threat engage their school. The SHELTR™ Training Program finally gives them all a chance. But to ensure the full power of the SHELTR™ Training Program is achieved we must all work together. That includes our schools, our communities, our government and our American companies and corporations.

American businesses interact with the American people every day. In order to effectively market to and increase the size of their sales demographic, American businesses have spent billions developing marketing strategies and marketing channels designed to reach the most people possible on a recurring basis. Billions more have been spent gaining the trust of the American people to ensure their recuring support of the products, systems or services being sold.

By partnering with our American businesses and corporations, The SHELTR™ Program can better reach the American people and more quickly earn their trust as we have partnered with the American Businesses they have learned to trust. This is an exciting opportunity for national, regional, and local companies and corporations to take part in school safety and to be an integral part of the School Security Solution.

In additional to American corporate partnerships, The SHELTR™ Program is working with the US Government to declare the month of August National School Safety and Awareness Month. By dedicating an entire month to school safety and security, American companies and corporations will be able to set-up SHELTR™ Partnership Programs and Campaigns. Some examples of national corporations and organizations supporting The SHELTR™ Program are listed below:

McDonald's – The entire month of August, Golden State Foods, Inc. will allow McDonalds to market a SHELTR™ school safety and security Happy Meal. Each Happy Meal box will detail security protocols from the SHELTR™ Program on the box and will have a toy related to the SHELTR™ Program.

Restaurants (Outback, I-Hop, Olive Garden, Etc.) – Restaurants across America will offer 10% discounts to all people that are ENSSA Members in the month of August.

Retailers (Wal-Mart, Target, Amazon, Etc.) – Retailers across America will offer 10% discounts to all ENSSA Members in the month of August. This also coincides with Back-to-School shopping across America.

Professional Sports – American professional sports teams show their support by wearing SHELTR™ Strong patches on their jersey's decals on their helmets, decals on their cars, boats, bikes, etc. The partnership campaign would be Athletes for SHELTR™.

By having this single SHETLR™ "Unified" School Security Solution it allows national corporations and organizations to be part of the school security solution.

# The SHELTR™ Program

## Declare "August" National School Safety Awareness Month

In order to bring awareness to issues facing America it has become a common practice for our US federal government to declare a day, week or month of awareness to that cause. We declare months as "National Awareness Months" to raise public awareness about significant social issues, health concerns, or cultural heritage topics, aiming to educate people, encourage discussion, and rally support for important causes by dedicating a focused period of time to a specific topic each month.

Key points of National Awareness Months:

- **Focus on specific issues:**

Declaring the month of August as National School Safety and Security Awareness Month brings recurring focus each year to school safety and school security in America. This also allows for concentrated messaging from our local and federal governments, national corporations, national organizations, local businesses, civic groups, churches and communities.

- **Increased visibility:**

By designating an entire month, the issues surrounding school safety and security get broader attention and can reach more people than a single day or week of observance.

- **Community engagement:**

A National School Safety and Security Awareness Month gives the proper amount of time for people to participate in events, fundraisers and/or volunteer for activities related to school safety and security.

- **Advocacy and policy change:**

Raising awareness can also lead to policy changes and increased support for addressing the important issues surrounding school safety and security. It provides a venue and platform for pushing forward the policy changes that are needed for more effective school safety and security.

# Notes

# Notes

Made in United States
Orlando, FL
04 November 2026

90203664R00024